My Mama Told Me

Motherly Wisdom for Everyday Living

. . . .

PeriSean B. Hall

MARIA,

THANK YOU FOR ALLOWING
ME TO SHARE WITH THE
WOMEN OF SHARED HOUSING!
LOVE & BLESSINGS!!!

Bolden Hall Publishing

All Scripture quotations are taken from
the following translations: King James
Version, New King James Version, New
International Version, English Standard
Version, Authorized King James Version,
New American Standard Bible, and New
Living Translation.

Library of Congress Catalogue Card
Number: SR 1-1292077271

ISBN-10: 0692273980

ISBN-13: 978-0-692-27398-2

Cover Design: Jon Kraynak

Editor: Judy Howard Ellis, Daybreak Lit

*To Mama, who loved me with her words,
her example, and her life. To my brothers, Percy and Patrick,
I love you dearly and may we always remember
and celebrate Mama, our treasured gift.*

* * *

Contents

Dedication   07

Foreword   09

Acknowledgements   11

Introduction   13

In Memoriam   15

1. I Know What It's Like   19

2. My Words About Mama   21

3. Mama's Words To Me   25

4. Mama On My Name   29

5. Mama On Forgiveness   33

6. Mama On Beauty   37

7. Mama On Motherhood   41

8. Mama My Helper   45

9. Mama My Biggest Cheerleader   47

10. Mama's Pet Peeves   49

11. Mama Steered My Course   51

12. Mama's Lessons My Blessings   55

13. Mama's Frequent Sayings   57

14. Mama On Men And Her Children   59

15. Mama On Trusting GOD   61

16. Mama On Tithing   65

17. Mama On Aloneness   67

18. Mama On Hair   69

19. Mama On Hygiene   71

20. Mama On Dignity   73

21. Mama Was Dying But She Ordered Me To Live 75

22. Mama On Remaining Calm In A Storm   81

23. Mama On Follow-Through   85

24. Mama On Leadership   87

25. Mama On Being On Time   89

26. Mama's Passion For Words   93

27. Mama Didn't Tell Me This   97

28. Salutation To A Mother's Courage   101

29. Kind Words About Mama   105

30. Mama Lives On   111

31. Mama I Remember   113

Dedication

"One of the most beautiful love stories in the world is the relationship between a mother and a daughter." —*PeriSean*

"A mother's love never dies." —*PeriSean*

I dedicate this book to the memory of my beloved mother, my best "Mommie," my best friend and my most trusted confidante. It is my prayer that the wisdom and love imparted in this book activate a catalytic change in and preservation of parenting God's way. This is not a perfect account of parenthood, but rather a noteworthy account of lessons learned by a daughter who learned from her mother's successes and failures. May this serve as tool that can be translated worldwide for generations to come and most of all for the greater good of God's Kingdom here on earth.

Foreword

Theresa Harvard Johnson

PeriSean Hall is by far one of the most amazing and godly women I have ever known. Hands down, God has blessed our spiritual sisterhood in ways only our Father in Heaven could ever fully explain to our hearts. In sister-ships like this, time and distance matter little when you are connected by Holy Spirit.

Reading this book only confirms the many conversations, smiles, laughter, tears, loving correction and words of wisdom that have passed between us – mostly on her part as she shared the lessons her mother taught at every opportunity God provided.

Those stories brought tremendous healing to my heart, marriage, relationships with my children, and friendships. They literally affirmed me as a woman.

I never met Saundra Kathyrn Bolden Hall, but I knew her in the Spirit through her daughter. My mother, though I love her dearly and consider her among the most courageous women in my life, was never able to mother me to the capacity she desired. Sickness claimed that relationship.

But it is the joy, love and wisdom between the pages of stories like these that give generations of people hope in an increasingly fatherless and motherless world. We need the voice of wisdom, triumph, and most of all, love.

Between each page of this book my sister Peri, as I lovingly call her, cries out in wisdom for all people, not just women, to hear the voice of reason through her own testimony of being fiercely loved even in the midst of truly dark days. There is no such thing as a perfected life – one free of trial and tears on this side of heaven.

But there is such a thing as perfecting love and embracing a heart that forgives and chooses to see the good in the midst of all the imperfections. Now that is God!

Peri's vulnerability is refreshing. It's not easy opening up your heart to strangers and giving them a glimpse into the most intimate parts of your life. I know Saundra Kathryn Bolden Hall would be proud.

I also know that each person who reads, MY MAMA TOLD ME: Motherly Wisdom for Everyday Living, will be challenged to examine their own lives and consider their investment in the next generation.

Peri teaches us that even when mistakes are made in life, wisdom commands that we adjust to do better, to become better and to expect more than what has been. She challenges all of those who have the honor of raising children to do so deliberately and with a godly plan in mind.

So I say, thank you Father for the life of Saundra Kathyrn Bolden Hall and what she instilled in her beloved daughter. My life and the lives of countless others will never be the same. Let the lessons learned lead us into Your loving arms.

Job 12:12-13 says, "Is not wisdom found among the aged? Does not long life bring understanding? To God belong wisdom and power; counsel and understanding are his" (NIV).

*   *   *

Acknowledgements

I thank God for my mother, Saundra Kathyrn Bolden Hall, because she left me a rich heritage: a spiritual legacy. She didn't have earthly riches, but she possessed abundant heavenly riches. Mama taught me how to love right, live right, and treat others right.

I'm proud to be her oldest and youngest daughter, as well as her pride and joy on this side of heaven. It has been a long, hard road without Mama, but she left me with great treasures. Her godly example. Her love. Her words. Her wit. Her wisdom. The most powerful gift I received from Mama was her witness of forgiveness, which saved my life.

I would also like to acknowledge surrogate mothers and mentors with whom I've been graced to walk through life. These women helped to mold me into ministry, marriage and motherhood:

Mother Lusety Ethel Marshall (In Memoriam)
Pastor Earline Martin (mentor)
Dr. N. Cindy Trimm (mentor)

*   *   *

Introduction

There is a cry in the land. It's the children's cry which emanates from God's cry. This cry is found in divorce, drugs, rape, incest, violence, suicide, abandonment, disrespect and neglect. The children are crying; can't you hear them? Where are the fathers? Where are the mothers?

For those who are crying, are they children or are they parents now? Perhaps both. We have children parenting children and adults who were never parented. What's going on and what went wrong? Can what was lost be found?

Where's that ancient wisdom that fortified the family unit? What happened to the safe, "filling-station brand" called family? What does it look like? What does it taste like? Some have never tasted; some have forgotten what it tastes like.

Wake up fathers! Wake up mothers! It's not too late. Even though you failed, even though you fell, it's time to get up because the children are crying, the children are dying. And it's time to awaken to wisdom.

"For the creation waits with eager longing for the revealing of the sons of God." (Romans 8:19, ESV)

* * *

In Memoriam

I wrote this book in remembrance of my beloved mother, Saundra Kathryn Bolden Hall. My mother had extraordinary gifts of expression, particularly as it pertained to words. This God-fearing woman had a supreme command of the English language and was widely known as a word connoisseur in her circles of influence.

She not only wrote well, spoke well, and taught well, but she loved and lived well. Mama taught me daily lessons through her words and actions. She was absolutely and wholeheartedly a Quintessential Mother!

When it came to parenting, Saundra Kathryn Bolden Hall was a gift to this world. That's why I wrote this book. I wanted to impart the wisdom that saved my life. I wanted to impart the love that this world desperately needs. I wanted to impart the lessons that have long been forgotten. I also wanted to make sure that my mother's legacy of love lived on!

Mother went home to be with the Lord on July 19, 2001, just two days before my birthday. She was diagnosed with renal carcinoma (kidney cancer) in February of 2001, and by the summer of that same year she transitioned home at the young age of 57. That time was so difficult for our family.

In fact, I still have times when I have to shake my head and accept the fact that my mother is at home. Yes, home. On this day, July 19, 2001, Mama appeared to me in a vision. She walked towards me and laid her head on my chest and said: "It's time to go home." Two-and-a-half hours later she passed from this life.

A few years after my mother went home, the Lord spoke to me in a dream and said: "Every mantle that was on your mother is now on you!" I was amazed because I knew my mother had many powerful gifts and talents.

She was a lover of people, a prolific writer, a consummate communicator, a brilliant musician, an innovative entrepreneur, an inspiring lover of people, and, most of all, she was a woman who loved God. She was truly a Proverbs 31 Woman.

Needless to say, I am a very proud daughter who is honored to carry the mantles that my mother was graced to carry. I owe it to my God and to my mother to execute, without apology, the authority and power He invested in me.

I must fulfill my assignment in the earth realm. My greatest desire is to please my Heavenly Father. One way I have done that is by answering the call to honor the memory and legacy of my beloved mother.

While I realize my mother was human and subject to the frailties and mistakes that we often succumb to as human beings, my purpose for writing "My Mama Told Me" is to tell the stories of how a God-fearing parent overcame seemingly insurmountable obstacles and yet glorified God with the way she lived and loved.

Mama was not perfect by any means. She made many mistakes just like all of us. But despite her mistakes, she was a model parent because she never gave up on her children, and she dedicated her life to nurturing them.

Now I invite you to sit back, open your minds and lay hold of the golden wisdom nuggets of a mother whose legacy isn't one of perfection, but one that remains relevant and timeless!

*   *   *

Notice (Disclaimer)

I am not an expert on parenting, but I'm certainly one who has been graciously parented by a mother who loved me with her life, all of her life. Thus in this account, my cry is to the parents who failed, or who feel like they're failing, and also to the recovering adult children of parents who failed. Please know that you can still make a positive impact on the lives of your children, your children's children and even other people's children.

Although this book highlights my parental experience with my mother, after many decades, I have been given another chance with my father who failed me initially as a parent. Today we have a loving relationship and share a mutual respect for one another. It has required a lot of work, but we have gained great dividends, and for that I'm truly grateful. He even gave me his stamp of approval for this book and that means a great deal to me.

Parents become better parents by hearing the cry of their children and by being attentive to their needs. Parents, your children will always need you – even if they don't know it.

Therefore, I urge you to connect or reconnect with the hearts of your children because a priceless, hidden treasure exists in the relationship between parent and child. The bottom line is: What do you want to leave with your children? What will be your legacy? It's not too late to build one. You can create a comeback legacy. I heard it said once, "It's not how you start, it's how you finish that counts." So finish well.

*   *   *

CHAPTER ONE

I Know What It's Like

I know what it's like firsthand to feel unsafe in your own home as a child. I also know what it's like to have a mother's love, comfort and protection – despite a dangerous and volatile home environment.

I know what it's like to have my childhood dreams of a perfect home shattered and to see the fabric of my family fall apart before my very eyes. But I also know how a mother's strength and courage to leave an abusive marriage gave my brothers and me the opportunity to hope for better, safer tomorrows.

I know what it's like to witness a parent threaten and jeopardize the life of the other parent. I know what it's like to put yourself in harm's way to save your mother from the hands of your abusive father. I also know what it's like to care for a parent who needs emotional support.

I know what it's like to see a mother press on and press through the devastation of physical abuse, divorce and lack. I also witnessed a mother's steadfast resolve to overcome the vicissitudes of life by choosing to be better and not bitter. Yes, I know what it's like to be parented by a mother who pushed past her pain to soothe the pain of her children and encourage their success.

Finally, I know a child's heart cry, and that cry is to be loved and cared for by both parents. I've seen the damage done. I have also experienced the victory won. Despite all odds, I am a child of the parented!

*   *   *

.

CHAPTER TWO

My Words About Mama

Mother wrote letters to facilitate change. Every time she wrote a letter, systems changed and transformed instantly. For instance, the financial aid department at my 20,000-student-plus college university shifted their financial aid disbursement policy after receiving a formal letter from my mother.

There was also a Texas Barber College that changed some of its policies, and a major department store that took notice of their customer service complaints. The list goes on. Change came because my mother wrote letters.

She was even quoted in The Dallas Morning News because of her response to an editorial column. Mom was also paid to write letters for people and eventually started her own desktop publishing business, The S Factor! It's no surprise that my brothers and I are all great communicators in our own right. I was proud of my mother then. I still am today.

When it came to music, my mother was a master. She started reading at the age of three and began taking piano lessons several years later. The organ was the instrument of her choice. She had a beautiful alto voice but refused to ever sing a solo because it made her too nervous. My mother began her career as a church musician at the age of 12 years old in Paris, TX, her hometown. Her music career covered a span of nearly five decades, until her untimely sickness and resulting death in 2001.

During the course of her career she traveled to New York to accompany her church young adult choir, she was church organist of several prominent black churches in Dallas, TX, a featured musician on a Dallas/Ft-Worth CBS-TV Affiliate church broadcast, the accompanist for prominent classical soloists and conductors, an organist who regularly played the Seven Last Words and The Messiah during Easter and Christmas seasons, and is also purported to be the first African American woman to play the pipe organ at the Meyerson Symphony Center, a concert hall located in the Arts District of downtown Dallas, Texas; ranked one of the world's greatest orchestra halls. These are just a few of my mother's notable achievements during her career as an organist.

All of my mother's gifts, talents and achievements were great, but most important to me was the solicited and unsolicited godly wisdom she imparted to me on a daily basis. She was the kind of personality and person that many intently listened to for intellect, wit and encouragement.

I have never known anyone who was more loving, loyal and forgiving. She was engaging, and people loved her for her warm and loving nature. Whenever she spoke, or entered a room, her presence commanded captive audiences. She was, among many things, a teacher, a comedienne, a lover of God and people, and a lover of life. I could not have asked God for a better mother because our relationship was very special; we were God's gift to each other. To say that I miss her is an extreme understatement. My two brothers and I were confident of our mother's unconditional love for us, and it was indeed God's agape love. God introduced us to His love through my mother, for God is Love and He is Eternal.

My parents divorced when I was in the fourth grade, and my father left my mother with three children to care for by herself. In spite of it all, Mother did not stop. She did what she never thought she could do alone: care for her three children.

Mom endured great struggles and heartaches along the way, but nevertheless, she took great care of us by making sure we lived in respectable communities, attended and graduated from the highest-performing schools in Texas, and supported us in our personal and professional endeavors.

During my mother's last days with us, I told her I believed she was the full expression of God's heart for motherhood. Mother at that time questioned her effectiveness and significance in life. I reassured her that if she did nothing else (which she did), she mastered motherhood!

I believe that is the greatest job in the world! I miss my mother more than I could ever express, but it gives me great joy to share her Legacy of Love and her Motherhood Mantle with the world.

I invite you to partake in the wisdom from my mother's heart and impute it in the hearts of your loved ones to live on forever. To God be the glory as I tell this story!

Allow me to tell this story because my burden of loss rolls away with each word I write, and it helps me keep my mother's memory and legacy alive. I believe that every person who reads this love story will be enriched, inspired, and encouraged by each nugget of wisdom. I am moved to say that my mother's words are forever etched upon my heart. Thank you, Lord!

* * *

CHAPTER THREE

Mama's Words To Me

Here are two letters written to me by my beloved mother. Over the years, I have read these letters to mothers and daughters alike. Mother's letters have inspired many as a result.

In fact, some of these women began writing letters to their mothers and daughters after hearing my mother's words to me. At the time of this first letter, my mother was very disappointed that she didn't have the money to throw me a 16th birthday party but she left me with something far more valuable: her love through her words. These letters from my mom are my most prized possessions in life. May Mama's words live on forever!

LETTER I: (My 16th Birthday) July 21

My Peri-thing,

Well, here goes the traditional "from-Mom-to-the-16 year-old" letter (smile).

The 16 years (has it really been that long?) that you've been with me have been among the best of my life. You've made the hard times easier, the sad times less so, and the "broke" times rich with your love and smiles. God knew I'd need you more than some other Mom-that's why He granted me you. I've done nothing to merit such a blessing; I can only be grateful. I can see beautiful years ahead for you, and will do all I can to help make them so, for your happiness is mine, also.

Ours is a very special relationship, one I hope we'll retain throughout our lives. I've waited for your "difficult teen years," but you've had none. Thank you, sweetheart.

I think, in these letters, Moms are supposed to impart some really great advice to their daughters. I think you already know what I'd advise: Hold on to God. In any situation, make sure He is first in your life. When times are good, thank Him constantly.

When times are bad, rely and lean on Him. Always know you're never alone, nor will you ever have a burden too heavy for you to carry. Remember the miracles.

Every step you make should be guided by Him. That's not to say you won't make mistakes or bad choices; but be assured that there's a reason for everything that happens, even the bad things.

Well, these are my words of wisdom to you, little loved one. I'm still trying to say "thanks" for sixteen of the most rewarding years of my life.

Stay as sweet as you are.

Be selective.

Be discreet.

Be helpful, polite and considerate.

Be self-preserving.

Be Happy.

Mama

*   *   *

LETTER II

Envelope reads: FOR MY VERY, VERY PERI

To My Daughter, at the celebration of her Thirtieth Birthday

What a wonderful day! What a beginning for you! That we should be alive to celebrate this miracle is a wonder to me! I almost (but not quite) have no words to express my feelings – of joy that you are my daughter; of elation at your continuing victory; of pride in your example; of sadness because you are no longer just my little girl; of thanksgiving that you have been just that; of awe at God's great Wisdom in choosing you to be one of the bearers of His message – so many, many feelings, yet so small a heart to contain them!

I remember you at so many stages- beautiful, shiny and new; as a more advanced baby girl, awakening all of us with your smiles; as a toddler – reluctant though you were to become one; as a "big girl" on your first day of school – and your last! And as a bride and wife, a remarkable, ever-blooming rose. Thank you for those memories, and all of the ones since, and to come. Your Nana and Papa are so proud! I just wish they could be here to tell you themselves.

Happy Birthday, Angel, and a myriad of more to come!!

I Love you,

Mommie

My mother used to tell me: "Peri, if you never did another thing, I would still be proud of you." She was not one for performance. I didn't have to "do" to win her love. She just "did" love and I knew without a doubt she loved me.

Now, let's hear more from Mama...

*   *   *

CHAPTER FOUR

Mama On My Name

My name, PeriSean is a combination of both my parents' names: Percy and Saundra. The "Per" in my name comes from the first three letters in my father's name, and the capitol "S" in my name is the first initial of my mother's first name.

My mother was a word connoisseur. She loved to work The New York Times Daily Crossword Puzzle nearly every day. She became a wordsmith by working crossword puzzles and learning the meaning of root words. One birthday gift my mother always gave me was a dictionary.

When I was in the third grade, my mother gave me "The Charlie Brown Dictionary." It was huge. I loved that dictionary, and I still have it somewhere in storage (I hope). When I went off to college my freshman year, she gave me a new "Webster's Dictionary."

As we both looked up "Peri," my mother pointed out to me the definition: a beautiful and graceful girl! She always told me that, but it was another thing to see those words printed in the dictionary. The dictionary confirmed that my mom was not making it up!

She also taught me another dictionary meaning of the word Peri, which meant the Persian Fairy. I also later discovered the Greek and Hebrew meaning of Peri, which means fruitful and abundant. The story of my name continues. My mother loved Irish and

French names, and she loved the idea of last names as first or middle names. The "Sean" portion of my name is both French and Irish and means "the grace of Jehovah" and "servant of God." Boy, I sure feel special, and I certainly have a lot to live up to. My middle name is Britton, which means "from Britain."

I don't recall a time when my mother didn't know the meaning of a word when asked. When I told her about discovering a new word, she would already know the meaning.

I was born during a time when there were no medical technologies in place that revealed the sexual identities of children. And somehow (I know it was God), when my mother became pregnant with me, she knew that I was a girl.

She already had decided that my name would be PeriSean. She decided to nickname me Peri while I was still in the womb, and even today all of my family and close friends call me Peri.

Having a unique name certainly has its challenges. I remember how my name was mispronounced quite often throughout my school years. Not one teacher in all of my 16 years of formal education was able to pronounce my name at first glance. Because so many people butchered my name throughout my adolescent years, it took me a while to like it.

But I can truly say now that I thank God for my name. I'm still growing into my name because it really gives me identity and value and a sense of belonging. My name authenticates me and my assignment here on earth. It also forever connects me to my Heavenly Father and my earthly parents.

It gives me hope and reminds me that I am deeply loved. My name is a constant reminder of who I am and every time I hear it, or discuss it, it's like music to my ears. Thank You, Lord, for blessing me with a name that provokes daily conversation.

People frequently ask me about my name. It gives me great joy to share the meaning because I will be connected to my mother through my name forever. The bond we shared here on this earth was amazing. It was truly like a beautiful dream from which I do not wish to awake.

Wisdom Nugget #1: Parents, take heed to what you name your children! When you name your children, you proclaim their destiny.

* * *

CHAPTER FIVE

Mama On Forgiveness

From my teenage years and into early adulthood, my mother saw in me a tendency to hold grudges. She frequently expressed concern that she didn't want me to live in unforgiveness. Mother understood the potential damage of unforgiveness.

She certainly knew what it was like firsthand to have her heart broken and to witness people in her life who willingly bore the wounds and years of unforgiveness and bitterness in their hearts.

Whenever my mother saw me exhibiting signs of unforgiveness, she would stop and correct me. She taught me by example and by her words. As a young child, I witnessed my mother being physically assaulted by my father on several occasions. I hated what my father did to her, but I didn't hate my father. Why? Because my mother didn't hate him. She did, however, provide another great example to me by divorcing him.

Mother had a quiet strength and beauty about her. When she experienced abuse at the hands of my father, she pulled herself together, checked on the three of us, and faced the world with courage once again. She told me many years later that she didn't desire to live during those miserable times of being a battered wife.

She went to counseling (in the 1970s); she was on tranquilizers, and she even dropped to 99 pounds at one time. She told me years later that when she fell asleep at night, she didn't care if she woke up. But each time she did, she knew the Lord wanted her to carry on and be there for her three children.

By the time I was in the fourth grade, my parents' marriage had fallen apart, and they finally divorced that summer. I can truly say that I never heard my mother say one negative thing to us about our father.

I have to say that it was because of my mother's forgiving spirit. We saw the beatings, and we knew our father was the culprit, but my mother never planted any negative seeds in us about our father. He was successful at that all on his own.

Of course, being the bright, keen and insightful children we were, we quickly arrived at our own conclusions, which was exactly what our mother wanted us to do. She did agree with us later about our findings, but encouraged us to forgive our father and continue to reach out to him.

I believe my mother quickly forgave others but had a harder time forgiving herself. After we became young adults, mother often apologized to us for failing to choose a good father. She would say, "No one could have ever told me that your father would have ever walked away from his children."

We didn't blame Mother for her marriage to our father, but I know it was hard for her to witness our pain because of the choice she made. Mama was hurt more over our pain than her own. That's a real mother. My mother's ability to forgive quickly amazed me.

When I was a young adult, a trusted friend of the family betrayed me. This incident greatly upset me. As soon as I got home, I told my mother about it. I just knew that she was going to be ready to rip this guy's head off. When I told her the guy kissed me (he was a minister), my mother took a moment and said, "Are you OK? He didn't hurt you?" I said, "Yes, I am OK, and no, he didn't hurt me."

After she heard my answers to those questions she said, "Baby, the devil works harder on ministers. I forgive him, and you must do the same." On the inside, I was like "What?!" But I could see the compassion my mother had toward this person. It was like she could see his struggle. I knew how much she loved me, and I also knew it had to be God who gave her grace and self-restraint.

Now one thing I want to say about my mother—she was definitely a "Mama Bear" when it came to her cubs—I know she forgave the guy, but I wouldn't be surprised if she called him to give him a piece of her mind. If I knew my mother, and I did, she probably threatened to harm him if he ever touched me again—but of course Mother never would have let me know she did that.

My biggest test of forgiveness came during the time my mother was critically ill with cancer. I was greatly offended by a private matter that occurred, but was unaware of how the offense had deeply affected me. My mother knew me all too well. I could never hide anything from her.

She also knew I was under great stress because I was her main caretaker and manager of her personal and business affairs, in addition to my own affairs. One day while I was talking to my mother in her bedroom, she told me she saw hatred on my face. Her observation surprised me.

I didn't know I was harboring hatred, but Mama saw it and called it out. Mother hated two things: hatred and evil intent. I knew she was not going to tolerate it in me. During this critical time in our family, I had a very dear pastor friend of mine, Pastor Rodney Stodghill, come over to pray with our mom and family once a week.

But that night, when Mama saw my hate-filled expression, she told me that the next time the minister visited, she wanted him to pray for me specifically! She said I needed to forgive, and she wanted me set free. Sure enough, the pastor arrived the next day. Mother informed him that he would be praying for me. He gladly consented to pray for my deliverance.

As the minister prayed for me, I opened my eyes to take a peek at my mother, only to find her staring right at me. She looked at me as if to say, "I will not be leaving this earth until you are delivered from unforgiveness, hatred or anything else that is evil!"

After I saw how serious my mother was about my deliverance (more serious than me), I decided to let it all go. I mean, there was no way I was not going to be free; I had no choice in the matter.

There are so many stories I could write about what my mother taught me about forgiveness, but the main thing I wish to convey is that she was very passionate about loving and forgiving people. She didn't allow even a hint of bitterness in her presence or in her children at any time.

This was truly God operating in her life because no iniquity dwells in His sight. Where He is, there is light, there is freedom, and there always is forgiveness. Thank you, Mom, for teaching me to forgive.

Then Peter came to Jesus and asked, "Lord, how many times shall I forgive my brother when he sins against me? Up to seven times?" Jesus answered, "I tell you, not seven times, but seventy-seven times." (Matthew 18:21-22, NIV)

Mother often reminded me of this scripture: "And the King will say, 'I tell you the truth, when you did it to one of the least of these my brothers and sisters, you were doing it to me!' (Matthew 25:40 NLT)

Wisdom Nugget #2: *When we forgive we are free. There always will be a constant need to forgive and to be forgiven. It's the only true way to freedom.*

* * *

CHAPTER SIX

Mama On Beauty

One thing I ask of the LORD, this is what I seek: that I may dwell in the house of the LORD all the days of my life, to gaze upon the beauty of the LORD and to seek Him in His temple. (Psalm 27:4 NIV)

My mother was the most beautiful person I have ever known. What made her so beautiful? Of course, it was the Light of the Lord that shined brightly in her heart and throughout her countenance. She smiled though she had plenty of reasons to cry or frown. She was quick to release whatever emotion she experienced at the time.

When she was jubilant, the laughter resounded and the tears flowed. When she was angry, the words spewed and sometimes debris flew. When she was sad, her beautiful eyes welled up with tears. Mother didn't hide what she experienced in the moment. She was real at all times.

Sometimes she struggled with depression due to her own fears and the sadness she felt because of her children's disappointments. Mother carried a lot, as many mothers and women do. Despite everything, she consciously chose to be content and endure with the love and grace of God.

She was beautiful because she was authentic and repentant; she was relational and giving, as well as loving and forgiving. Throughout the many years and months before her untimely death, I was privileged and honored to observe my mother as a highly skilled and anointed organist. I recall many Sundays when she played along with the choir, and the Spirit was really high. Mother would raise her right hand to praise the Lord as she played the organ with one hand and two feet.

After the song, she would be drenched in tears. She never tried to hide them; she would just let her tears flow. As she did, her beauty broke forth. I admired my mother's tears and her courage to be who she was.

Mother also had her fears. One of her fears was really surprising. As a classical organist, she trumpeted many a pipe organ. But there was something wrong with how she responded to this amazing instrument. It was not the beautiful instrumentation of the pipe organ, but the sound this machine produced when she turned on the pipe organ.

The resonating pipes terrified her so much that she refused to be alone as the organ warmed up. Oftentimes, someone started the organ for her before service. Again, this is another example of how authentic she was. She didn't disguise her phobia.

I remember the time I started to "smell myself" (get the "big head"). I was in the 10th grade at that time. I said things like, "I'm this, I'm that," and when Mom heard enough, she said, "Stop that! Don't let me hear you bragging on yourself like that again." I soon learned that boasting was a pet peeve of Mother's, and that was something I'd better not do in her presence and not at all. Besides, Proverbs 27:2 states, "Let another praise you, and not your own mouth; a stranger, and not your own lips." (ESV) Mom taught me that true humility is beautiful and boasting is prideful.

Many people remarked on how beautiful my mother's smile was. I mean her smile lit up any room. Mom's smile was merely a reflection of the beauty contained within. Her smile was infectious, warm, inviting and very loving. With her smile came a very beautiful, deep laugh. Laughter is a sign of a merry heart. My mother had many heartbreaks in life. Because she allowed her heart to break, I believe her heart became pure and strong. She bowed when she was broken, and that's what kept her pliable and resilient in life and in her dealings with people.

Her tone of voice also denoted love. She had a warm and soothing speaking voice. Whenever she spoke, people listened intently. I never saw anyone who could command the ears of a room full of people the way she did. Many people sat at her feet to listen and laugh.

Mother didn't yell, at least when it came to me and most people. My brothers, on the other hand, well, that's a different story! My mother maybe raised her voice at me a few times during our years together. As a teenager growing up, there were a few times when my mother said in a calm voice, "Peri, I'm very disappointed in you."

It broke my heart because hearing those words come out of my mother's mouth was worse than any whipping or yelling I could have ever received. She was a person I longed to please the most because she was a reasonable, sensible and loving person. She was someone you never wanted to disappoint.

Mother was simply beautiful in her dealings with people. It was paramount how she treated others and she taught us to be kind and polite to everyone. When my mother raised her voice at someone besides my brothers, she was defending her children. She was very protective.

Everyone who truly knew her realized that if you ever wanted to get on her bad side, just mess with her children. Mama was less likely to defend herself that ferociously, but she wouldn't hesitate to defend us when she believed it was necessary.

I also saw how my mother protected the beauty and innocence of others. Our choir was visiting at a Dallas church when I noticed my mom lingering around the sanctuary after the service. She was observing the interaction between an older man and a young girl. The young girl was visibly upset every time this man spoke to her.

My mother was livid! To my surprise, she began loudly asking around for the pastor. Mom did not stop until she made it to the senior pastor's office to let him know that a child was being abused in the sanctuary. I was amazed at my mother's passion and persistence in getting this matter handled; and that she surely did!

Wisdom Nugget #3: *True beauty must have its full expression. It cannot be hindered, held back or clogged up. It was born to be released. There are no bounds to beauty. So, let beauty bountifully abound!*

* * *

CHAPTER SEVEN

Mama On Motherhood

To me, my mother's greatest strength and beauty were in being a mom! I remember her as loving and nurturing. She told my brothers and me she loved us every day and kissed us with love every night.

We even had to kiss my mother goodnight when we called ourselves being mad for getting punished for something we'd done wrong. There were a few nights we tried to go to bed without saying goodnight because we were angry.

Boy, Mama didn't let us get away with that. As we headed to our rooms, fuming, she would sweetly and softly say, "Come, kiss me good-night." We knew we had to turn around and give Mama a kiss and say goodnight, no matter what. She never let us go to bed angry with her or anyone else.

All of our elementary, junior high and high school friends loved to visit our home because my mother was so warm and receptive to them all. They enjoyed being around her because they knew she cared about them as individuals.

The hardest day to try and get my friends to go home was the day after my slumber parties. My friends just wanted to hang around my house. My mother laughed with them, listened to them, and engaged them in conversation. She treated them like gems. I had such an awesome relationship with my mother, and for a while, I was oblivious to the fact that this wasn't the case for many of my friends. I soon learned in my formative years that what my mother and I shared was rare.

I had friends who didn't get along with their mothers. They took my mother into their confidence and talked with her because they trusted her. Mom was a communicator, and she allowed us to express ourselves openly, but respectfully.

Many of my friends were able to do this with my mom as well. Mother helped them to understand themselves better, and she helped them to understand their parents from a parent's perspective. Both our friends and their parents loved and appreciated my mom for this reason.

One of my fondest childhood memories was when I was about five years old. I'd gotten sick in the middle of the night and thrown up. My mother was right there to take care of me. She brought me a 7-Up and sat with me until I felt better. Mama stayed right by my side, and it made a world of difference.

There were times that she couldn't fix things, but she always said, "Baby, if Mama could fix it, I would." In 2000, I went through a traumatic divorce and afterward I had difficulty releasing the trauma. One Saturday morning, I woke up feeling a bit shaky.

Later on that day, mother called me. When I answered the phone, she knew something was wrong. She had an uncanny ability to detect when something was wrong with me by the sound of my voice. I suppose it's that "Mother Radar."

When she asked me what was wrong, I was speechless. She knew then that she needed to get over to my apartment quickly. Whenever she came to visit me, I listened for her footsteps as she made her way to my door. I was like a little girl who was filled with such joy every time I saw my mother.

She entered my apartment with her arms extended, and we embraced as we headed toward the couch. When she sat down, I sat on the floor in front of her. She held her arms out again and asked: "What's wrong?"

When I proceeded to tell her that I was having difficulty releasing the pain from my divorce, I suddenly burst into tears in her arms. I cried and cried and cried until I could cry no more. My Mama just held me. After some time, I looked up at her and began laughing hysterically.

As I fixed my gaze upon her, she reminded me of Princess Leah from Star Wars. Her hair was styled like Princess Leah's with a part down the middle and one pinned pony tail on each side. Her hairdo was not as neat as Princess Leah's that day. As I continued to laugh, I managed to tell my mother why I was doing so.

She said, "Baby, when I heard you over that phone, I knew I had to get here fast." And then we both laughed. I miss the laughs we shared so often.

I miss her presence because she was there for me in the good and bad times. I could always reach her when I needed her. Now I feel her love with me, but I truly grieve the loss of her physical and emotional presence – even after all this time.

I remember dating this guy my freshman year in college and telling him off one night. I felt so bad about the things I said to him that I cried. I called my Mama (spoiled, I know) to tell her what happened and she could hear how upset I was.

She asked me, "Baby, would you like me to come and get you?" I said, "Yes." It was after 11 on a Thursday evening and Mom was about 40 minutes away. My mother came and rescued me.

Every time my mother came to campus, all of the kids who knew me would call her "Mom!" She was sweet to everyone and they loved her. Mom and Debra, a good friend of mine from college, usually talked for hours. Debra would call for me and then end up talking to my mother the whole time. Days later my mother told me, "Peri, Debra called." Wow. So much for having my own friends!

Wisdom Nugget #4: *Motherhood is a high calling filled with great rewards. I believe one of the biggest rewards God will hand out in Heaven will go to the mothers who captured His heart in their parenting. My mom is certainly one of them! Congratulations, mothers!*

*   *   *

CHAPTER EIGHT

Mama My Helper

I remember when I had my first big heartbreak my junior year in college. During that experience, I lost my self-esteem and became very depressed. One night I told my mother over the phone that I didn't have any reason to live.

I could hear in her voice how she wanted to come through the phone. She said to me, "Don't ever let me hear you say that again. You have everything to live for!"

She told me to call the university the next day to schedule some counseling sessions. Now, you have to understand, my mother was a pioneer. She was advanced in knowledge, education, mental health, and many other disciplines.

When she went through a traumatic divorce in the 1970s, she consulted with a white counselor, which was unheard of in the black community at that time. Back then, and even now in some cases, black people didn't believe in going to see counselors.

I believe my mother was one of the first brave ones to seek help in this way. She was a trailblazer indeed, and she was well-informed about other cultural and social means for advancement or assistance.

Counseling changed my life because I benefited from my mother's vast experience with it. To this day, I keep counselors around me – first and foremost the Mighty Counselor!

My mother, like any mother, never wanted her children to experience pain. Mama knew there were some things she couldn't fix for me, but she was wise enough to direct me first to the ultimate source: God. Then she recommended counseling as a resource.

After all, the Bible states in Proverbs 11:14 (NKJV): "Where no counsel is, the people fall: but in the multitude of counselors there is safety." I'm so glad I had a mother who didn't steer me wrong. I even learned from her mistakes as a parent because she admitted when she was wrong and apologized.

Wisdom Nugget #5: *Parents desire to heal the pain in their children's lives, but when they can't, they identify the Source Who can. His name is Jehovah Rapha.*

* * *

CHAPTER NINE

Mama My Biggest Cheerleader

My mother was always there to help me pick up the shattered fragments of my life. When my father abandoned me as a young child, she consoled me. When I felt flawed and unattractive, she told me, "You are beautiful."

When I was all alone, she supported me in all that I did and believed. I can't help but believe that my mother knew what it was like to be me. That's why she had such compassion and understanding.

As I mentioned before, one of my favorite things my mother said to me on a regular basis was: "Peri, if you never did another thing, I would still be proud of you."

That statement still blesses me today. Because of my mother, I felt accepted, cherished and loved unconditionally. Even when she was angry with me, I knew she loved me and would never turn her back on me. My Mama affirmed me by telling me I was going to make a great mother.

She saw how I loved and nurtured my niece Peyton, who was an infant at the time. I would hold her, kiss her, teach her and be very patient and loving toward her. One day when Mom and I kept Peyton, she had a crying spell. My mom picked her up to comfort her, but Peyton kept crying. When I picked her up, all the motherly love

I had flowed out of me. She stopped crying. Peyton and I shared a special bond, but that tie was there because of the love my mother gave to me and to Peyton. It was truly a gift from God!

I remember when I sat beside Mom at her sickbed. I was angry at someone for not supporting me emotionally during that difficult time. The LORD spoke to me in that moment and said: "You see the LOVE you and your mom are experiencing right now?" I said, "Yes." He went on to say, "(name) will never know this kind of love." Immediately, my heart broke for this person. Compassion and forgiveness sprang from my heart.

I am so thankful to the Father for His unconditional love that flooded through my mother. Because of His love through her, I will always know the deepest kind of love; I will always know HIM. Amen.

Wisdom Nugget #6: *Children feel so empowered when they know and believe both parents love them. When they receive unconditional love, children believe they can conquer the world.*

"What, then, shall we say in response to these things? If God is for us, who can be against us?" (Romans 8:31 NIV)

* * *

CHAPTER TEN

Mama's Pet Peeves

Mother often came to her children's rescue. Part of that rescuing included correction. She was a Music and English major in college and how fortunate it was for us that we benefited from her areas of expertise. Mom was always on a mission to correct our grammar.

We could hardly get our sentences out before she revised our speech. She corrected us in love, and that vastly increased our learning curve. Her older sisters were in on this too; they corrected us, and I know they corrected their own children. Mama knew the importance of speaking well and wanted us to be at our best.

She was the type of person who would whip you (with gentle words and, sometimes, a belt) and heal you at the same time, but the by-product always was healing. You felt the cut. But Mother applied the balm so quickly that before you knew it, you were bandaged up.

Just as the Lord instructs in Proverbs 3:11-12 (NASB): "My son, do not reject the discipline of the LORD, or loathe His reproof, for whom the LORD loves He reproves, even as a father corrects the son in whom he delights." Mother would rather you be angry with her for correcting you, than to see you walking around embarrassing yourself, or her (smile).

Another one of my mother's assignments in life was to correct ill-mannered behavior. Mother despised uncouth behavior. We would be quickly sent out of the room and possibly punished because of it. We weren't allowed to belch out loud, break wind, or stomp away angry.

Lord help us if we ever slammed a door in her house! She taught us to be polite, to say "thank you" and "excuse me," to tell the truth and apologize when we were wrong.

This seems pretty basic, but in today's society this appears to be a lost art. I believe we should revisit the old school standards. That's another reason why I wrote this book.

We were taught to love and honor our elders and leave the room when adults were having a conversation. Mother seemed to know the right time and place for many things in life and was fully committed to imparting these ideals to her children.

Mom also hated to hear mispronounced words. That was a serious pet peeve of hers! You may not be doing it on purpose, but the very act of mispronouncing a word grated on her nerves.

The worst-case scenario was when someone tried out a newfound word on my mom. Now my mother had the most extensive vocabulary of anyone I have ever known, and if you were coming to her with a new word, you'd better know the appropriate pronunciation, definition and usage.

If not, you stood to lose word credibility with her fast! Many people admired my mother's word prowess and aspired to be like her in that regard. But there is one big difference: Mother not only "knew" words, she had an anointing for words. God stamped her as a word specialist! And she certainly reigned in her lane.

Wisdom Nugget #7: *God commanded parents to nurture, train, teach and correct their children with their words and by their example. There is a distinct difference between a child who simply "grew up" and a child who was "raised."*

CHAPTER ELEVEN

Mama Steered My Course

Somehow my mother knew the path I was to take in life, even though I wanted to run in the opposite direction. It was the summer I was promoted to the eighth grade.

I had received my teacher assignments for the new academic year, and I was extremely relieved to find out that Mrs. Phenora Brown would not be my eighth grade English teacher.

You see, my brother Percy was in her class the previous year. It was through him that I found out that she was teaching Freshman College English to eighth graders! Mrs. Brown was also the only black teacher at our middle school.

This was a school where over 90 percent of the students were white. Many parents wanted their children in her class because it was a college preparatory course.

But that wasn't important to me. The rumor going around school was that Mrs. Brown's class was hard. I wanted to avoid that. I also didn't want to be in Mrs. Brown's class because my brother Percy was one of her favorites.

I didn't want to live up to the high expectations that he set, or be compared to him. Needless to say, when my mother got wind that I was not in Mrs. Brown's English class, she said, "I'm going up to the school to put you in Mrs. Brown's class." But Mama didn't stop there. When she got to the school, one of the school administrators told her about an elective speech class (which I was also trying to avoid) that was open. Mama enrolled me in that class as well.

Yes, Mama made me do the very things I was trying to avoid, especially because these things involved English and speech. Please understand, before that experience my mother allowed me to participate in decisions that affected my life because she knew me to be a wise and precocious young girl.

But this time, I didn't have a vote! Mama was in charge, and she did not budge. I worked very hard and did well in the classes. My mother knew the greatness in me even though I tried to hide it because of my shyness. I'm so glad Mom pushed me to go further than I could imagine.

Being in Mrs. Brown's English class was a great learning experience for me after all. She was very inspiring! Most of her students didn't know they would be going to church every time they attended class.

They didn't know that she was actually a preacher. Mrs. Brown taught English as if she was preaching a sermon. She was passionate about English and passionate about her students' learning.

It was funny to watch Mrs. Brown teach, and my classmates' reactions were priceless. Each student witnessed Mrs. Brown experiencing a "Hallelujah moment" when someone answered a question correctly. White students jumped or look stunned at the jubilation Mrs. Brown exhibited. They would flinch and gaze at her, amazed and puzzled. Everyone loved her, though, including the parents.

I will never forget Mrs. Brown. The writing and language skills I honed in her class still benefit me today. The speech class was also a blessing. Isn't it funny how parents know how to guide their children's lives?

Mother was also very instrumental in helping me get on track in college my first semester. I had decided my senior year in high school that I would major in business because I was good at accounting.

I soon discovered during my freshman year in college that just because I was good at something didn't mean that it was something I was destined to do. It hadn't ever occurred to me that I could enjoy my work.

One day I had a discussion with my mom about my college studies. I told her I wasn't doing well in my economics class and that I intended to drop it.

Mama could tell I was not happy, so we had a talk about what I really wanted to do. She told me that my work didn't have to be laborious. In fact, she told me my work was meant to be something I enjoyed. Mother reminded me that I excelled at sports casting.

I was a huge Dallas Cowboy enthusiast, and I knew the game well. Mom said to me, "Why don't you go into broadcasting?" I was flabbergasted. That's exactly what I wanted to do, but I didn't know it until that moment.

That conversation with my mom shifted the course of my destiny. Needless to say, I immediately changed my major and I was well underway to a happy career in Radio-TV-Film production.

Wisdom Nugget #8: *Parents hold the wheel that steers their children towards destiny. GOD simply requires parents to hold onto the wheel while He steers it. This ensures a progressive journey and an ultimate destiny that gives GOD glory and the beneficiaries much success.*

* * *

CHAPTER TWELVE

Mama's Lessons My Blessings

Mama told me: A woman's reputation follows her wherever she goes. A woman's reputation once ruined is difficult to repair. Carry yourself like a lady. Keep your head up. Never let me catch you with your head down.

Head up and shoulders back. Save yourself for your husband, she said. He will enjoy every facet of you. A man wants a wife he can trust to safeguard his heart.

Always keep interests of your own. Put no man in God's place in your life. God created you to have your own identity and significance in Him.

I know the lessons my mother taught me didn't simply come by osmosis; she learned many of them firsthand. She paid the price of a battered wife and a divorced woman with three children who sacrificed time and rest because she worked long hours to keep them fed, housed and loved.

She paid the price of being a black professional and hard-working woman in a white, corporate-driven society. She paid the price of a failed judicial system who refused to grant her child support because my father's attorney convinced the court he couldn't work. She even rallied residents of apartment communities to expose the unjust practices of leasing companies. She endured persecution on jobs because her intellect, self-confidence and fortitude threatened upper management. She was a woman who not only bore her own pain, she shouldered the pain of her three children – a burden simply too hard to carry in the end. Mama was tired. She fought a good fight. All of her life.

Just over a year before my mother's passing, she witnessed the pain of my very public and traumatic divorce. Nonetheless, mother's faith in God never wavered. She continued to lean on the LORD.

Her love and hope for her children never ceased. In fact, her love and hope increased. You see, these lessons didn't come cheaply. Although they were numerous, she taught them with grace, pride, humility, respect, forgiveness and love.

These are the reasons why I have to salute my Beloved Mother! She was a Champion by God's grace and mercy. She failed, but she was a winner! She's still winning. So are we!

Wisdom Nugget #9: *Parents, be aware: Your children are always paying attention to the voluntary or involuntary lessons you teach. Many times lessons learned come from being burned, so any parent's lesson learned can be a child's wealth earned.*

* * *

CHAPTER THIRTEEN

Mama's Frequent Sayings

My Mama told me: People are generally good. People aren't perfect and don't expect them to be. Give people room to make mistakes.

- Don't be so hard on yourself.
- Don't cast pearls before swine.
- If a dog will bring a bone, he will carry one.
- Don't let your left hand know what your right hand is doing.
- Keep your word. Follow through.
- Be professional and never let your adversaries see you sweat.
- Always hold your head up and your shoulders back.
- With each day of life, God gives us a clean sheet of paper to write on.
- Mind your own business.
- Love the elderly, respect your elders.
- Remember who you are. Don't be puffed up.
- Show love, care and concern for others.
- Forgive those who mistreat you.
- Don't ever let me catch you mistreating anybody.

- Don't let the sun go down on your anger.

- Always look and do your best.

- You are beautiful.

- Examine yourself.

- Don't judge others.

- Lend a helping hand.

- Laugh.

- Wear a smile.

Wisdom Nugget #10: *Mama knows what's best for her nest. Listen to her and honor her.*

"The wise woman builds her home, but a foolish woman tears it down with her own hands." (Proverbs 14:1 NLT)

CHAPTER FOURTEEN

Mama On Men And Her Children

My mother became a single mom in her early thirties. She had no moral, emotional or financial support from our father so she made the brave decision to take care of herself and her three children alone.

Mother had good-paying jobs because she was brilliant and talented. She was a legal secretary by trade, a church organist, and, at one time, she held three jobs because she wanted the best for my brothers and me.

Mama didn't believe in depending on a man to help her care for her children. She knew that if she had dated a man who contributed money to our household, then he might have expected to have a say-so in the lives of her children, and that was absolutely out of the question!

My mother was not a "neck worker," but she was a "Homey don't play that" type when it came to her children. She dated a few men over the years, but most of them weren't introduced to us.

For the men we met, I'm happy to say that none of them ever spent the night, lived with us, abused her (or us), and none of them disciplined us.

Besides, we were good kids and our mother loved us more than her own life. She protected and shielded us as much as she possibly could, especially me, her only girl.

I didn't mind though because I always knew it was because she loved me. I did, however, have to learn some hard life lessons later on because of my sheltered lifestyle. But that's another book.

I will always be grateful to my mother because she put her children first. Now it's understood (according to biblical principles) that if she had married, then her husband would have come first. But this was not necessarily the case with my mom. As things were, we never had to wonder if she would run out on us when the next bus (man) came along.

We never had to compete for her love and attention. And we certainly didn't ever have to wonder if she would take our word if someone had violated us in some way. She always invited our opinions and never questioned our word, unless someone had proven they were a liar.

Mother always cautioned us to tell the truth and warned us about the consequences of telling a lie; she defined a lie as not telling her the whole story. I thank God for the kind of mother who protected her children.

My mother never remarried, but she came close twice. The two "candidates" just did not measure up. It takes a real king to find and appreciate a queen and my mother was indeed a queen!

Wisdom Nugget #11: *Parents honor their children by making them feel loved, valued and protected at all times.*

"And, ye fathers, provoke not your children to wrath: but bring them up in the nurture and admonition of the Lord." (Ephesians 6:4 KJV)

* * *

CHAPTER FIFTEEN

Mama On Trusting God

My mother knew the Bible—especially stories about the relationship between David and Jonathan, Noah and his sons and lessons on how to treat your brother, your neighbor, etc. She often used to quote the hymn "Father, I Stretch My Hands to Thee."

Mama believed in the Almighty God and the power of His Word. She trusted God in the direst of circumstances. For instance, on the eve of her surgery to have her left cancerous kidney removed, we discovered she had a bladder infection.

That Sunday, my mom went to the bathroom and couldn't pass urine. She alerted me. I went in the bathroom and knelt and prayed over her. Mom could see that I was near hysterics because I saw she was hemorrhaging—she calmly said to me, "Baby, God's got me!"

Her ability to comfort me and trust God amazed me. She could be in the midst of a personal trauma but if she saw me freaking out, she always would have the strength to calm me with her touch and her soothing and loving voice. I'm sorry, but when it came to the safety and health of my mother, I stayed on overdrive. I believe my mother knew that.

Here's another instance when my mother taught me to trust God. Our family needed a financial miracle. I was in middle school when mother was laid off from her job. We had no way to pay rent or buy food. At that time, we lived in an upscale townhouse community in Richardson, Texas.

My mother didn't qualify financially to live in that community, but because she had the favor of God on her life, the landlord granted us access. It's good to know people in high places, and we did. Most importantly, we knew the Most High. My mother always had favor with people in leadership positions. They were either partners in high-powered law firms or department heads of corporations. She either matched or superseded their intellect while remaining humble and gentle as a dove. I believe this is why her gifts and personality brought her before great men and women.

Now back to the miracle. The dreaded eviction notice was delivered to our door. After we received the notice, my mother looked at me and said, "Let's go pray." I don't' know where my brothers were at the time, but when it came to prayer, my mother always made sure I was in on the meeting.

We proceeded upstairs to my room to pray and fell down on our knees as we held hands and sought God for our much-needed miracle. We also had a few friends that were praying for us. It was not long after we got up from our knees that our doorbell rang.

When we opened the door, we saw a caravan of people from an area church who had brought us boxes of food. My mother and I just looked at each other in amazement. Of course, my mom started to cry. Mother expressed her emotions freely. Me, on the other hand, I had to remain in control (tough) because that's the role I took on early in my childhood.

After the group brought in all the groceries they presented us with a check that covered our rent. It was at this time that I began to realize that God really does answer prayer.

I can see now that my mother was teaching me life skills way back then. She taught me to trust, lean and depend on God during the good and the bad times.

I'm so thankful to my mom because the lessons she taught me prepared me for many of the things I have faced in life, and her love and support guided me through them all. I know that she's still with me, cheering me and my brothers along in life.

Mama, I salute you for teaching me to look to God to be my everything. You didn't just teach me, you showed me how to trust God. I know your rewards are great in heaven. Thank you!

Wisdom Nugget #12: *Always trust God in the highs and lows of life. Stay with Him through it all because the King in you always rises to the top!*

* * *

CHAPTER SIXTEEN

Mama On Tithing

I remember my first job. I was 14 years old and in the ninth grade. I was thrilled because Mother gave me permission to buy my own school clothes.

My first job was with a catering company. I had to wash, iron, and fold hundreds of tablecloths and napkins. On occasion, I even had the family working with me.

We had a three-ironing-board system that worked. It was me, my mom, my dad (when he visited us), and sometimes my older brother. We all knocked out those loads of laundry fast.

Two weeks after my first completed assignment, I received a paycheck. Boy, was I excited! That was until my mother said, "Peri, you know you need to tithe, Baby!" I thought, "Aw, man!"

Tithing was the last thing I wanted to do. But because I was a child who valued my mother's instructions, I immediately complied. I wasn't happy about the concept of tithing, but I obeyed.

It seemed to work in my favor. After that time, my mother reminded me to tithe during every job until she saw that giving back to God had become a habit for me. I was a good manager of money. I believe my mother saw that ability in me at a very young age. No one taught me how to handle money in my family. I just did it.

Mom often said I inherited that gift from her father and older sister because neither she nor my father knew how to manage money.

As I look back, I see how my mother was helping me to cultivate my gifts by making sure that I put God first. She knew that as I dedicated the first tenth of my earnings to the Lord, He blessed the rest.

Wisdom Nugget #13: *Tithing ties us to God. When we tithe, we are connected to God and His promises for our lives.*

*   *   *

CHAPTER SEVENTEEN

Mama On Aloneness

Never have I known a person who loved being alone more than my mother. She was very comfortable with solitude, and she spent most of her adult years alone. When I say alone, I mean without a mate.

Mother would visit her favorite spots like bookstores and fashion resale shops by herself. She enjoyed meals alone and savored long, solitary hours of reading. She was never bored. She remained content! She had a full, happy life.

As I observed my mother over the years, I learned that being alone was a good thing. Because of her example, I never felt like I had to have a man in my life even though for some of the women I knew, it seemed to be a necessity.

I refused to settle for anything or anyone just to avoid being alone because I, too, enjoyed my own company. During my college years, some "friends" criticized me for not having a man.

Most of the girls I knew during that time all had boyfriends, and a few of them thought something was wrong if you weren't dangling from a man's arm.

I fell in love with a couple of guys during my freshman and sophomore years in college, but not for long. I simply was not ready for a committed relationship and neither were the guys that I dated. Besides, my focus was earning my degree. I knew I wanted to marry eventually, but I didn't meet the right guy in college, and I was only just beginning to learn me. Consequently, I remained drama-free and stress-free for the remainder of my college years. I'm glad my mom taught me that it was OK to be alone because that lesson helped me to become me.

Things were a little different for me when it came to friendships with women. I had a great relationship with my mom, but I also desired other friendships with girls my own age.

I didn't have many friends, and I didn't understand why. Nor did I appreciate the separateness I experienced at that time. I first took notice of this separateness in high school. I tried to join certain cliques, but they never accepted me.

On top of that, I didn't care to be around some people in those groups because I was selective. In many cases I just didn't fit in, and as a result, I lacked close friendships for many years.

The harder I tried to have a group of girlfriends, something always happened, and I ended up alone. This made me very sad. I didn't understand. I knew I was a nice person and fun to be around, but why was I alone when it came to friendships? Why couldn't I have one buddy?

I did have a buddy here and there, but again, I always ended up alone. I finally stopped fighting the aloneness and accepted that perhaps this was God's will for me.

This was hard to understand because I was such a people person. During my senior year in college, I began to notice that whenever I was alone, I heard God's voice. I soon learned that aloneness was a calling.

Wisdom Nugget #14: *Being alone is not a death sentence. It's an invitation to gain intimacy with God and an opportunity to explore self-discovery. There is no true oneness without aloneness.*

CHAPTER EIGHTEEN

Mama On Hair

Hair was a valued commodity in my household, particularly with my mom. Her hair was always nicely styled, very thick, beautiful and hi-ho silver!

As a little girl, I remember going to the beauty shop every time my mother went. I remember how good it felt to have a fresh, pretty new hairstyle each week.

The beauty shop experience elevated my self-esteem and showed me that my mother cared about the way that I looked. Thanks to my mother, I still value and take good care of my hair.

We all know that there is such a thing as a bad hair day, right? Well, I watched my step around my mother whenever she had a bad hair day. Each time she prepared to go anywhere, such as church, work or a formal event, it was important to her that her hair turned out right.

If her hair was not right, then her whole attitude soured. I remember being there sometimes as she readied herself for her outings. I hated when her hair didn't turn out the way she preferred because she would get angry and throw down the comb. I would think, "Uh, oh!" when her mood soured because of her hair.

But my mother's hair looked beautiful to me, no matter what! She had a lovely head of hair and was well known partly because of her hair. Mother wore her hair short, medium and long. In the 70s, she even wore an afro and wigs. No matter how she wore it, people loved her hair. So I learned early on that taking care of my hair was a priority.

When I was in high school and college, people said to me: "We never see your hair messed up." They were right. My hair remained perfectly styled, and I didn't like people to touch it. One day during my freshman year in college, we had a tornado warning.

I had just washed my hair. I was just getting ready to style it when the tornado alarm went off. We had to evacuate the dormitory via the stairwell. I lived on the eighth floor at the time. I tell you, it was a long walk down those flights of stairs, especially for me. My hair was all over my head.

I was embarrassed and humiliated. This was a lesson in humility. I knew I wasn't perfect, but I never wanted people to know that my hair wasn't! I had to get over myself and realize that most people didn't even notice me or my hair because we were all concerned about an impending tornado, which, by the way, proved harmless.

Wisdom Nugget #15: A woman's hair is her crown of glory. A crown should never provoke a frown. Mothers, teach your daughters to care for their hair because caring for their hair makes them self-aware.

* * *

CHAPTER NINETEEN

Mama On Hygiene

I remember when I started my menstrual cycle at age 13. My mother cried because she knew her little girl was growing up. After she had wiped away her tears, the first thing she said to me was, "You know you are a woman now, and this means you can have babies." She continued, "This is not a license to have sex, and I really encourage you to wait until you are married."

All I could think about was, "Wow, I'm a woman now!" I was so proud. I did make a mistake early on during my pathway to womanhood, though.

I remember when I accidentally left a balled up "sanitary napkin" (that's what my mother called it) on the bathroom counter we shared. She kindly called me over and said, "Don't ever let me see you do this again."

She spoke to me gently but yet firmly about the importance of cleanliness. She taught me how to dispose of a sanitary napkin properly, and keep myself exceptionally clean during this time. Mother always communicated with me openly.

There wasn't anything we could not discuss. She always wanted me to know the proper names and pronunciation of words, and, in particular, she wanted me to say the word "menstruation" correctly. She said that many people mispronounced this word, but she was going to make sure that I didn't.

Personal hygiene was very important to my mom. She followed the strictest hygiene regimen, and she made sure the three of us followed suit. In addition to bathing on a regular basis, she always flossed her teeth, washed and styled her hair and made regular visits to the doctor and dentist.

I believe my mother knew that good hygiene was a reward to self and a gift to others. After all, her hygiene habits kept her body in good working condition and promoted high self-esteem. She always looked great, smelled great, and treated people great. Excellent hygiene has it rewards!

Wisdom Nugget #16: *Hygiene seems basic and fundamental, but many do not give enough attention to it. Personal hygiene management promotes good self-esteem and fosters good, interpersonal relationships.*

* * *

CHAPTER TWENTY

Mama On Dignity

Never let them see you sweat and always hold your head up high. Never let your enemies see you cry. My mother knew that our enemies delighted in our losses, especially if they witnessed them firsthand.

Most of our pain as a family was public, as were our lives in many ways. My mother's divorce, my divorce – we were frequently on public display in the church. That's just the way it was.

Once in the midst of a church service, mother was having a hard time dealing with the pain of my very public divorce. When I noticed she was starting to break down and cry in front of everyone, I persuaded her to step out of the service with a trusted friend. She knew this was best because this is what she taught me.

We didn't keep up appearances, but we displayed a sense of class and dignity because that's who we truly were. I've found out through these experiences that public tests challenge us to become our best. I remember my mom talking to me about my posture when I was in the ninth grade.

Mama told me to walk with my head up and my shoulders back. By the way, I represent a lineage of family members who have the longest and straightest spines. Our spines are as straight as ironing boards.

I know this is because many of us have been trained to walk in an upright manner and to walk worthy of the calling we have received. Despite being knocked down in life, God built us to get straight back up.

Even in death, my mother held her head up straight toward heaven as her spirit ascended to the Lord. I am grateful that she left me a legacy that says, "As you look up you will go up!" She was indeed the epitome of royalty.

Wisdom Nugget #17: *Although life knocks you down, you are divinely designed to get back up. You find dignity in trusting and knowing that God will pick you up, no matter how many times you fall. When you remember who you are, you will be a shining star.*

* * *

CHAPTER TWENTY-ONE

Mama Was Dying But She Ordered Me To Live

My dear, sweet mother even took care of us during her last days on this side. Unbeknownst to me, she told a couple of my friends who visited us during the time of her illness to watch out for me.

Mama wanted them to be there because she knew I would need them when she died. She accepted that fact long before I did. I didn't want to accept that she was leaving me, and I didn't want to face abandonment again.

After all, I had already been abandoned by my father, then my husband, and now my mother. Mama was tired of the struggle of bearing her burdens. She was tired of watching her children tirelessly take care of her.

The night before she passed, she asked me, "You all must be tired?" I said, "We may be tired physically, but we will never get tired of taking care of you."

I knew deep down that my mother decided that night it was time for her to go home. She didn't want to burden her children any longer. She also knew that I would take care of her for as long as she needed me. The only place I wanted to be during that time was right at my mother's bedside, and that's where I was until her dying day. I cared for my mother, and she cared for me, even on her sick-bed. I remember one night when I awoke to check on my mother.

That night when Mama looked at me she noticed that my T-Shirt was wet with sweat. She reached over and grabbed my shirt and told me to change because she didn't want me to catch a cold.

I felt so loved during that moment because in the days and weeks before, my mother silently seemed to detach herself from this side of life. I couldn't believe I was losing a part of her while she was yet still with me. Mother faced her impending death head-on. She met with her Maker and communed with Him daily as I sat alongside her bed.

Approximately one week before my mom's passing, I asked our dear friend, Pastor Rodney Stodghill, to pray with our mom at her bedside. Pastor Rod is a "heart talk" specialist, and I wanted him to pray a heart-talk prayer with my mother.

During that prayer, he asked her to let Jesus hold her. I knew Jesus was present because when I looked at my mother, I saw her transition her heart into heaven. It was clear that she had transcended to another realm.

As she laid there in Jesus' arms, Pastor Rod asked her what she saw. Mama began to describe heaven. She said she saw a silver lining, and then she told us that she danced with Jesus. We were all amazed and speechless. Mother truly saw heaven that day, and we were blessed to have been a part of it. I know for myself that heaven is real!

I rarely left her side during the five months before her passing, but Mama often encouraged me to go out and get some air and sun. This great woman encouraged me to live even when she was dying.

When I wanted to die, and I wanted to, she encouraged me to continue. After all, I had suffered through a failed marriage just months before and now, worst of all, I had to face the harsh reality that my mother was leaving me. She was the only person I knew who loved me, and now God was taking her. I angrily wondered, "How could this be?"

My mother saved my life before she left. When I accepted the fact that she was leaving me, I decided to no longer serve God because I had been through too much already. I felt He had let me down and I was truly angry with Him.

One night as I sat at mother's bedside, I asked her what I was going to do without her. My mother gathered her strength and said to me: "Keep your hand in God's Hand. I will always be with you, but in a different way."

Those were the prophetic words the Lord spoke to me through my mother that saved my life. When I heard those words, I sensed I was closer to God than ever before. I knew then that I would not be walking out on God. Not then and not ever.

I never told my mother about my plans to turn my back on God, but somehow she knew. I also knew she would not allow that to happen. Thank you, Mama, for saving my life!

Wisdom Nugget #18: Mothers are life-givers and life-savers. When a mother uses her words as a life-line for her children, the impact is immediate and eternal. May the breath of God continue to blow life in and through all mothers.

On the day of my mother's passing, I had a dream. In the dream I saw my mother come to me and say, "It's time to go home." She was telling me she was going home to be with the Lord. After I had awakened, Mama went home to be with the Lord two and a half hours later.

A few years later, I was inspired by God to write the song, "Mommie's Home," which I wrote in about 15 minutes. This song was birthed from my mother's words and my deepest grief:

"Mommie's Home"

VERSE:

I can't believe the thing that I feared most has come true,

My mother's gone home and I don't know what to do,

You see we shared so many precious years,

And held each other through our tears,

What in the world do I do now?

What do I even say?

I don't even want to pray.

VERSE:

Cause I spent the last few years serving God with all my heart,

How could I know that mom, my Mommie, would soon depart?

You see, I thought she'd always be with me for this my eyes could see --

But when I saw her leaving me I knew it had to be.

CHORUS:

"Mommie Said"

Keep your hand in the Master's Hand you see,

He's the One that keeps you and me,

You see, I'll always be right in your heart for we will never fully depart --

And I'll be right there to greet you home when God says, "servant, well done."

BRIDGE:

I'll never leave you, I'll never forsake you,

I'll be with you until the end,

For I'm your God, the Only Wise God --

Just Trust in Me, and I'll see you through.

OVERLAY:

I'll always be right in your heart,

For we will never ever depart,

I'll be with you until the end,

Through thick and thin,

I'll never leave you,

Won't forsake you.

Lyrics and melody written by: PeriSean Britton Hall, copyright 2005

*   *   *

CHAPTER TWENTY-TWO

Mama On Remaining Calm In A Storm

I'm still learning this lesson. Mother always said to me, "Peri, don't project ahead!" She knew that I strived for perfection, which caused me to worry when things didn't work out. I always paid my bills on time, kept the best credit and straightened people out in a minute when they crossed the line with me.

I appeared to have it all together, and I thought I was in control! But deep down, mother knew I was at times a very scared little girl. There was a time in my life when all I did was worry because our world as a family was out of control.

I learned to worry about things when I was a child because my environment was full of domestic violence and uncertainty. I wanted to be sure that my family was safe and that we had what we needed to survive.

Anything that seemed to threaten my perfect little world set me off on a worrying tangent. As a child, I wondered how we would pay the bills, whether my mother would be safe from the hands of my father, and what would happen to me if I lost my mother. I voiced these concerns to my mother.

She quietly replied, "Peri, everything will be fine. Don't worry." Ever since I was a little girl, I imagined having a perfect family with a perfect life where nothing went wrong and everything was right. I knew I did not want the life my family had then.

I also remember complaining – right out of college – about the high interest rates of credit cards. This got on my mother's nerves. I even voiced my concerns about tomorrow, next week, next month, and beyond. I admit, when things didn't go the way that I had planned, I had a tendency to become rattled.

God told me once, "Keep your mind out of my business." Sometimes I have a tendency to over-think and over-do things. The Lord is still teaching me that He is in control, not me. I'm also one of those people who is hard to surprise because I'm always expecting something great to happen – but the problem is, I think I know how it's going to happen.

I'd like to think of myself as an eternal optimist, but there are times when I fear the unknown or the unexpected. For instance, one time I lost my cool when I heard my mother fall. This occurred during her battle with cancer.

She had been very weak and bedridden. Late one night my brother Percy and I were watching TV at my Mom's house. We heard a thump upstairs. I knew it was her. I ran upstairs and found my mother on the floor. I lost it.

When I saw my mother lying flat on her back, I thought she was gone. I wasn't ready for that. My brother Percy picked up my mom and me off the floor that night.

After I regained some composure, I noticed that my mother, who appeared to be OK, was comforting me. She looked stunned to see me so shaken. Mama told several family members the next day that I went berserk, which I did. But it was also the first and last time I had lost control during that time.

The Lord stays my hand these days. He makes sure that I trust Him one day at a time. He knows me just as He knows all of His children. He has the solution and the treatment plan for anything that we may battle. Thank God for that.

But I have to admit, I prefer being "in the know" when it comes to the basic things in life. When my mother was fighting cancer, I was trying to avoid the faith walk by living only by what I saw.

God had a different plan because He was training me to live in the faith realm – the only place where I have experienced GOD. I had to learn to trust Him for a place to live, food to eat, for health, strength and other things I took for granted.

I learned a lot about faith in God from my mother because she was the most trusting, forgiving and loving human being I have known. When we lacked the essentials, she knew how to pray and believe God for what we needed.

She encouraged me to do the same. The fact that my mother could comfort me, knowing she was leaving this green earth within weeks or days, amazed me. Mom trusted the Lord all the way to heaven. Her faith never failed. And neither should ours. That is one of the most powerful lessons I learned from my Mama!

Wisdom Nugget #19: *Trusting God means believing He will catch you when you fall. Trusting God means knowing you are always in His hands, and He's got it all!*

*   *   *

CHAPTER TWENTY-THREE

Mama On Follow Through

D o what you say you will do! Finish what you start. Be consistent. My mother did these things: She prayed, loved, read, worked crossword puzzles, taught her children valuable lessons, kept her word to people and finished whatever she started, even during sickness.

Mother always chastised me because as I began to mature into adulthood, I had the bad habit of starting things and not finishing them. I would sign up for the latest multi-level marketing campaign or the latest healthy-living plan and within a few days or weeks I was off to something else.

Each time I came to mother about my latest venture, she would say to me, "Peri, now you know that you will no longer be interested in that within a few days. Are you sure you want to get involved?" I'd say, "Yeah Mama! This is great!" And sure enough, Mom's prophecy proved to be true sometime later.

Thanks to my Mama, I have learned to be true to my word, honest with myself, and honest with others. She said if your word is no good, your name is no good.

Isaiah 55:11: "So shall my word be that goeth forth out of my mouth: it shall not return unto me void, but it shall accomplish that which I please, and it shall prosper in the thing whereto I sent it." (KJV)

Proverbs 22:1 also speaks to this: "A good name is rather to be chosen than great riches, and loving favour rather than silver and gold."(KJV)

Wisdom Nugget #20: *Your word is your bond. If your word is no good, then you are rendered ineffective and powerless. When you back your word, you pack your power.*

*   *   *

CHAPTER TWENTY-FOUR

Mama On Leadership

My mother was a church organist for most of her life. What she learned about leadership she learned first and foremost in the church. Because of her leadership role in church, she, like other staff members, interacted with the pastor and his family more often than many members.

She also communicated with the church's governing boards, which, at times, involved politics. Through this governing system, she observed the role of pastors and other people in appointed roles.

Her attendance at church business meetings and involvement in church committees gave her an inside look at how leaders conducted "church business." These experiences helped her to later advise others about respecting church leaders.

Believe it or not, some parishioners had no regard for the pastoral office because many of them saw pastors strictly as men with a "headship title." Even though these pastors were in fact men, Mama came to see them as more than just men because she saw how God's presence heavily guarded them.

It was important to my mother to follow and support the direction of appointed leadership at all times, whether in the church or in the workplace. Now, this did not mean that she never questioned leadership, it just meant that she carefully honored her leaders.

She remained careful and prayerful about how she addressed the leaders in her life, and she taught me to do the same.

Mama witnessed some of the most unfavorable consequences of irreverent behavior toward God. Over the course of a few years, my mother saw on several occasions what happened to people who were known for opposing the pastor openly and irreverently.

It was not a pretty picture. Some of them fell ill and a few died suddenly. This isn't to say that this is always the consequence of such actions, but it can certainly serve as a warning.

I am mindful of what happened to priests back in biblical times when they irreverently and presumptuously touched the presence of God. They fell dead. (2 Samuel 6:7, AKJV): "And the anger of the LORD was kindled against Uzzah; and God smote him there for his error; and there he died by the Ark of God."

During those times, when priests went before God on behalf of the people, if the priests were unsanctified before God's holy throne, they fell dead. In a similar way, mother taught me that touching pastors or other leaders with words from my mouth, or by showing disrespect, God would see this as touching and mishandling His presence. She reminded me that people err because they believe they are attacking a man, when, in fact, it's God they are offending.

Even though in today's world we live under the Covenant of Grace, we are not exempt from the penalties or even casualties of mishandling God's presence. The consequences bring forth death, whether physical, spiritual, or relational. When we kill another man's harvest with our words or behavior, we kill our own.

Wisdom Nugget #21: Recognize and reverence God's presence in or around a man or woman in leadership. A leader in position represents God's authoritative presence. To irreverently challenge the man or woman in position is to jeopardize your own well-being.

CHAPTER TWENTY-FIVE

Mama On Being On Time

When it came to arriving places on time, my mother was a specialist. Not only was she on time, she was a little early too because she hated rushing. She hated being late to anything, and she didn't waste time with people who were habitually tardy.

In all her 45 years as a church organist, she never was late to church or choir rehearsal unless it was beyond her control or if there was an emergency. It is clear that timeliness was important to my mother because she consistently honored God, valued her time and other people's time by making sure she was on time for everything.

My mother also taught me the importance of being thoughtful and considerate of someone else's time and feelings. She told me on a regular basis that the world did not revolve around me and to maintain a state of thanksgiving.

Another important lesson my Mama taught me was to not "keep your company waiting." She told me that if I was riding to an event with someone, I needed to be ready when they arrived. She told me that their time was just as important as mine, and if I were on someone else's time, I shouldn't keep them waiting.

Another reason my mother valued being on time was because she witnessed how latecomers drew attention to themselves when they arrived at church or other special events.

Oftentimes these were people who made a grand entrance and were unaware that God's sanctuary wasn't a place to draw attention to oneself. My mother wasn't a person to make appearances. She always tried to remain low-key and did everything within her power not to draw attention to herself.

One of her greatest pet peeves was self-promotion. And for my mother, the "spirit of lateness" was a type of self-promotion. I believe she interpreted that type of lateness as, "My greatest concern is myself."

Mother also saw how some people drew attention to themselves because of a contribution they made to a particular project or cause. For instance, she saw how self-promoters became upset and outraged because their name was left off a program. She also saw how they became outraged when no one publicly recognized them or their achievements.

After seeing so much of this kind of malarkey, my mother decided that whenever she contributed to a project of any kind she wanted to remain anonymous. My mother was very innovative and over the years she wrote and designed programs for weddings, funerals, theatre plays and other special events.

When it came to printing these materials, she always left specific instructions to leave her name off of programs. At other times, she just had the name of her business printed, which was The S Factor. During her final days on earth, I saw to it that my mother made it to her last doctor's appointment on time. I drove Mama to her appointment that day and we were running behind schedule because I had difficulty helping her get dressed and to the car.

When we arrived at the doctor's office, she told me to drop her off in front of the hospital building. I obeyed. I went in to secure a wheelchair for her and a hospital attendant came out to wheel her into her doctor's office while I went back outside to park the car.

My mother was very ill and very weak, but she made her way into that doctor's office on time. I saw that day how much timeliness meant to her.

In her last words to me, my mother said: "It's time to go HOME." I praise God that she was on time for that as well.

Wisdom Nugget #22: *Don't underestimate the importance of timing because there is a pre-set appointment for every tick on the clock. Don't be late for your pre-appointed date!*

* * *

CHAPTER TWENTY-SIX

Mama's Passion For Words

No one loved words more than my mother. She had worked her crossword puzzles from the time before I was born until the time she went home to be with the Lord. I'm not talking about just any crossword puzzle. She worked The New York Times crosswords puzzle.

This was her daily activity and favorite pastime. She could sit all day with her crossword puzzles, pencils, pens, dictionary, a book, her favorite TV shows, popcorn, popsicles, her glass of diet soda and have herself a good time.

Mother studied root words and let me in on a little secret. She told me if I knew the origin of a word, I could figure out the meaning of any word.

My mother knew that words had power. Whenever she spoke, she commanded the attention of people no matter where she was. She had mastered the English language and her soothing and reassuring tone won people over. She was an English and music major in college and her college education certainly paid off.

For Mother, words were especially important because she was a music artist, as well as a word artist. She valued the importance of articulating song lyrics clearly. If you ever wanted to get on her last nerve, then mispronounce a word. I mean she would really become vexed in her spirit.

For my mother, it was just as bad hearing a choir mispronounce words during a song as it was in simple speech. Mom pointed out to me that one word church choirs frequently mispronounced was the word "worship." She hated hearing choirs sing "worshup." I mean, she hated it. She would point out to the choir director that the choir needed to enunciate the word as WOR-SHIP, not WOR-SHUP!

Mother was a music conductor at heart; a maestro for sure, even though she refused to stand before a choir or orchestra to conduct. As a young child, I remember being gently awakened by the resounding classical music that traveled throughout our house every Saturday morning.

I would awaken to find my mother joyously waving her arms with precision and in syncopation to select classical pieces of Beethoven, Chopin, or Bach. Just as she waved her hands in fluid concert with the music, she was the same way when it came to proper word usage.

As beneficiaries of her mastery of words, mother routinely corrected her children's language usage, whether we were talking or singing. I was given a few lessons on the pronunciation of certain words in particular. The word "often" was one word I regularly mispronounced.

Whenever mother heard this, she would say, "Peri, the word is pronounced 'ofen' not 'often'; the 't' is silent." She also corrected me when I said, "Psalms Chapter 1," for example. She would passionately say, "Peri, it's Psalm Chapter 1," which meant I needed to drop the "s" at the end of psalm. Sometimes I was hesitant to speak around my mom because I knew she listened to every word I said and how I said it.

Even though it frustrated me at times, I wanted to be right. I wanted to sound intelligent and educated, just like she did. And I must say, all of her hard training is paying off!

I can say that she molded me into a grammarian as well, along with my two brothers. We don't know it all, but we do know when to do our research! Dictionaries and thesauruses are powerful tools.

Because the three of us became quickly sensitized and thus familiar with words and their proper usage, whenever we ran across a word that we weren't familiar with, Mother would instruct us to look it up. Now she knew the meaning of the word, but we realized later that she wanted to pass along her passion for words. When I really think about it, I don't remember a time when my mother didn't know the meaning of a word.

To say she had an extensive vocabulary is an understatement. I believe the woman could have written her own unabridged dictionary. After all, she worked crossword puzzles for over 40 years of her life. She was an impressive, prolific wordsmith and writer to say the least.

As a matter of fact mother came from a family of Word Doctors! Whenever her sisters came to visit us, they spent plenty of time correcting our grammar.

We got to where we didn't want to say anything around them because they corrected us so much. But now we all can look back and see how valuable the correction really was.

Wisdom Nugget #23: *Words are powerful instruments designed to inspire, correct, teach, construct and heal. When used correctly and carefully, words can be a healing balm to the hearers.*

"The Lord GOD hath given me the tongue of the learned, that I should know how to speak a word in season to him that is weary: He wakeneth morning by morning, He wakeneth mine ear to hear as the learned." (Isaiah 50:4 KJV)

"Let no corrupt communication proceed out of your mouth, but that which is good to the use of edifying, that it may minister grace unto the hearers." (Ephesians 4:29 KJV)

CHAPTER TWENTY-SEVEN

Mama Didn't Tell Me This

O ut of all the wonderful things I learned from my mother, there's something very vital I never learned from her...

Mama taught me how to love, but she didn't teach me how to be loved. You see, the household in which I grew up, I tended to the needs of others to feel safe as a child.

When Mother suffered abuse at the hands of my father, I assumed the role of taking care of her emotionally and protecting her because whenever she was in danger of being abused, I became very afraid. Afraid of what, you might ask?

As a child, I feared losing her and being left alone. Therefore, I dreaded the possibility of being abandoned by another parent. That was more than I could bear the thought of at eight years old, or any age for that matter.

The fear of losing my mother drove me to care for her excessively, and, later on, to care for others to the point of losing myself. I learned to program my behavior and my emotions to be directly attuned with my mother's responses to the violence or stress she experienced.

I stayed on guard, proactively anticipating my mother's every need. If she was sad, I comforted her. If she cried, I cried too. When she was tired from working, I tried to make her comfortable with house shoes or a cooked meal.

I made it my business to keep her safe, and I believed as long as I was around, she would be. But this was not always the case. This protective behavior continued throughout my childhood and into my post-college years.

For many years, I remained preoccupied with my mother and family's needs and didn't realize how out of touch I was with my own – until I experienced a nervous breakdown.

My preoccupation with my family's needs and my marriage at the time, left me feeling sad, empty and afraid. Again, I was losing my sense of self. My family had grown accustomed to needing me because I made sure I was their hero; the "hero child". Well, being their hero got me to zero, and I've walked in great freedom since that time.

The tables shifted the year I had my breakdown. All of a sudden, my family was caring for me. When I got back on my feet some nine months later, I began to learn how to care for and love myself. I'm still working on this.

As a child, I wish I hadn't been placed in the position of caring for a parent, but it was how I survived my environment, and perhaps it's even one way my mother survived. As an adult, I have made the mistake of neglecting my own needs to attend to the needs of others.

I wanted to satisfy my need to feel safe, loved and needed. But I soon found out I was still not satisfied. This codependent behavior only left me feeling empty and depleted. It seemed I didn't get it until I experienced a few more bumps on the head. Those bumps became my cues to get back to "me."

Because I am a people person, I have to remind myself of what happens when I lose myself in the lives of others. Once I remember, I get back on track! This is something I will have to continually work on to maintain a balance. I've learned to accept the fact that self-investment is necessary, and it's OK.

What good has come from this experience? I have learned to be a very caring and loving person who stays keenly in touch with the feelings and dispositions of others.

I have a childlike, playful nature that I enjoy, and it keeps me fit and young. Through learning to be me, I acquired the art of journaling and this keeps me in touch with my real self. I have learned how to serve others and serve myself first with the same passion and fervor.

Wisdom Nugget #24: *Self-care is a necessity. Caretakers: When you care for others and neglect yourself, you will end up needing intensive care. Give yourself permission to care for yourself in some way, every day.*

* * *

CHAPTER TWENTY-EIGHT

Salutation To A Mother's Courage And Strength

The courage and strength to trust her God and step out on faith. The courage to be alone and raise her children alone. The courage of becoming a woman of great wisdom and intellect. The courage to endure public scrutiny and ridicule because of the "D" label (Divorced) she was assigned by society.

The courage to be her children's protector and provider. The vulnerability of being alone, yet not allowing herself or her children to be overcome by predators or predatory systems.

The courage to move beyond being a victim to a victor. The courage and strength to overcome critics and naysayers. The courage and strength to fight for what's right and to right and cite wrongs, albeit verbally or in writing.

My mother was this woman. She protected her eldest child from his abusive father, a man she deeply feared during their 9 1/2 years of marriage. When my father decided one day that he wanted to manhandle my brother instead of whip him, it was my mother who moved into harm's way to protect her son.

I will never forget that day. While my brother was being whipped by my father, I heard my brother say, "Leave me alone, I hate you!" My father began to roll up his sleeves, and as soon as he did, my mother stepped in between her child and this man. I saw a new, brave and bold woman emerge that very day.

That day later sparked an event in her life when this same woman, after over nine years of marriage and three children, decided to divorce her abusive husband and raise her three children alone. For many years, that same woman worked three jobs and a great deal of overtime to take care of her home.

Our lives and lifestyle continued to improve after my mother divorced my father. We were not devoid of struggle, but we were free from fear and terror, and we regained peace and happiness in our home. We lived in the best of neighborhoods, attended the best schools and lived in a safe environment, all because Mama decided to trust God alone.

Throughout my life with my mother, I saw a woman who loved deeply, was hurt much and forgave all the more. I am reminded of my mother (and me) when I read Luke 7:47-48: "Wherefore I say unto thee, her sins, which are many, are forgiven; for she loved much: but to whom little is forgiven, the same loveth little. And He said unto her, thy sins are forgiven." (KJV)

Mama was hurt in part because of her own bad decisions, and she was hurt by hurting people who chose to hurt others. But all these experiences spurred her on to love and forgiveness. Somehow, she was more forgiving of others than she was of herself – in one particular instance, at least.

The fact that my father failed her three children troubled her the most because she saw the negative and painful impact his absence had on our lives. Even though her children were fatherless, she lived with them and loved them through their pain.

Mama wanted to remove all our pain but realized she couldn't, which is what hurt her the most. I do believe, however, Mama was able to forgive herself eventually.

I'm glad I knew a woman who made decisions that set us on the path toward our destiny. Whether we get there is up to us, but my mother's strength in quietness, gentleness and meekness helped pave the way.

I honor her for showing courage in defending and supporting the weak, standing up for what she believed, and, most of all, I honor her unwavering faith in God.

Wisdom Nugget #25: *Mothers are instinctively full of strength and courage. Many times this strength emerges when they sense their children's need for protection. I pray that this same strength and courage will enable mothers to love, protect and forgive themselves.*

* * *

CHAPTER TWENTY-NINE

Kind Words About Mama

One of the first times I had the privilege of a sacred glance into heaven was serving my sister, Saundra Hall. Cancer was squeezing the ebb of life out of her body but her heart and spirit were very much alive.

She allowed me the joy of being with her and we walked together into His presence, just for a moment, to taste of what was to come for her in a few weeks and a few years for me.

We were praying together and she began to rock back and forth on her bed. I asked her what is happening. She smiled, and said, "I am dancing with Jesus." The smile, the rest and the joy arrested my seminarian trained mind and I simply enjoyed His presence in her life in that moment.

She opened her eyes and her daughter said that the peace that filled her soul on that day carried her through the next few days until the Lord called her home.

What I tasted, the glance that I got into heaven, the peace that was in my heart, carried me through the storms that would enter my life in the next few years.

Betrayal of a good friend and disciple would be the cancer that would enter my soul and seek to steal the ebb of life that lived in me. The peace of Christ now gives me a safe place to retreat to and hide. No matter the pain, no matter what tomorrow may hold, I know He will be with me and I know I will dance with Him and later with my sister, Saundra Hall."

—*Pastor Rodney Stodghill*

"Saundra Hall was one in a million. Her beauty was breathtaking, her intellect was astonishing and her artistry was genius. She was as comfortable with the elite as she was with the common man. Her love for life was infectious. I was blessed to know her as both a friend and confidant."

—*Selmore Haines III*

She was a beautiful, warm loving mom with a big heart. She made me and my husband feel so welcome when we moved to Dallas. She took to us like we were her kids. I also remember her smile and her fabulous silver hair! Thinking about her now makes me miss her and you too, Peri!

—*Juli Ann Harkins*

Peri — your mother was beautiful and sweet! I didn't know her well, sorry to say. When I saw her, we were always at Jackie's, watching the Cowboys.

I remember her sparkling eyes, her bright smile and silver hair. Times could be tough, but she always, always, always was positive, smiling and up beat when I was with her.

She had a wonderful laugh. You and I had not met, but she spoke so fondly of you and your brother. Seems that her qualities have been passed down lovely lady!

—*Margaret Lake*

Friends come and friends go. Real friends, may leave but there will be foot prints on your heart forever. My best friend ever will be in my heart forever. Love her and miss her so very much.

—*Mary Ann Armstrong*

Always loved my "other Mother." Be blessed!

—*Troy Marsh*

Saundra was a Great Lady and a good friend to my mom.

—*Robert R. Estell, Sr.*

Peri, I thought of Aunt Saundra today! She will always have a special place in my heart. I miss her dearly!! My Auntie Saundra had a way of soothing the soul, not only with her touch, but just by being in her presence. She always made me feel loved and welcomed in her home. She would greet me with a heartfelt hug and was genuinely happy to see me whenever I visited. She would make me laugh out loud with her sense of humor.

When I was going through the tough and emotional teenage years, she would always be willing to listen and offer sound advice about love and life. Redrick misses her bright smile and laugh and how supportive she was about our marriage and decisions. She told us how much love she felt when she visited our house. Love u Cuz!!

—*Stephanie Johnson*

Yes indeed! Beautiful inside and out with a smile that would light up a room.

—*LaTara Thompkins*

Vision of Saundra Hall:

Shortly after Saundra Hall passed away, the Lord showed me in a dream that she was dancing in heaven with her mother. It was like the scene in the Color Purple. They had joined hands and were moving around in a circle dancing and rejoicing. I knew without a shadow of a doubt that it was her mother in the dream with her.

—*Debra Glasco Jones*

I never shall forget her playful, wise cracking spirit! And talented!!!!!!! Girl gave an instrument a hard way to go!

—*Myrna Beckett Burnside*

She was a wonderful lady! Always had a kind word to say!

—*Angela Abney Herron*

I remember her beautiful smile and hair. Also I remember her playing the organ. I know you miss her so much but I am sure she is so proud of you.

—*Jennifer Fincher Walters*

PeriSean what a beautiful picture I can remember her looking like that with that smile just like it was today. Thank U for sharing her with us. God Bless You.

—*Johnnie Marsh*

I miss her as well! She treated me as if I were part of the family. She was beautiful inside and out!

—*Horace Myrick*

Your mom, the musician, the bibliophile, the wordsmith, my dear friend. I cherish our time together occurring in both college, church and our many telephone colloquies. WHAT AN INCRED-IBLE LADY cum HUMAN BEING! You replicate her well!

—*Eva Flowers*

*   *   *

CHAPTER THIRTY

Mama Lives On

My mother died, but yet she lives. She's alive in Christ Jesus and in the hearts of those who love and remember her. She was one of God's best, and she is deeply missed.

Mama has passed the baton to me, and it's time for me to carry on where she left off. Mama entrusted her entire estate to me, and that didn't just include her material possessions. She trusted me to practice and teach what she taught me. She trusted me to continue in love and forgiveness.

She trusted me to continue to be kind to others and self-preserving. She was also confident that I would continue my walk and dance with the Lord. Her hope for me was that I would find happiness, peace and contentment on this side of heaven.

Her expectation was – and is – to greet me and other family members and friends on the other side when the Father says, "Well done thy good and faithful servant." And with God's help, we all will.

Those who encounter me know that my mother remains very much a part of my life; death can't take that away. Nothing will replace the love we shared.

My hope is that this love will be multiplied in others. As I share memories of my mother with others, the pain of losing her physical presence lessens, but joy increases as my tears flow.

So be patient with me because this is what I need to heal, to feel, and be for real. I have committed my life to becoming the woman God created me to be, and I have Mama's example ever with me to see! Thank you for letting me share my Mama!

Pass it on!!

WORD POETRY

For my mother, words were surgical tools that were carefully chosen and properly utilized at the right times in proper spaces of specified places. Words comprised a language that created moods that halted or sparked attitudes. A woman of graceful words, Mama was a voice that many heard because she spoke and everyone listened.

An entertainer, Mama's ability to hold the attentions of others defied description. She loved in word and deed and attended to many needs. Her temperament was calming and assuring, always exuding hope that was enduring.

A woman of many tears and much laughter, one could say she was a "Word Pastor." A very passionate woman was she, filling her atmosphere with glee. Wherever she went, her light shone as bright as the Heavenly Master's throne.

Many were attracted to this light, as her home was flooded with late calls at night. Pleas for help, pleas to be heard, she was always there to serve. Mama always loved...Mama was loved.

* * *

CHAPTER THIRTY-ONE

Mama I Remember

Mama, I remember your unfailing love, which only came from above

I remember how you loved and cared for the boys and me, as well as your friends and extended family

You never turned hurting people away; always providing a listening ear each and every day

To me, you were the most beautiful woman who ever lived, giving your life so faithfully to the ones you held so dear

Your smile and laughter brightened many a day; people knew you to be no other way

Your presence brought such great cheer as it illuminated the lives of those who were near

You traveled on buses, trains and planes and this is where you always took the time to proclaim the Master's Holy Name

You were a Worshipper and Chief Musician who loved God, you played that pipe organ with passion-filled laud

You were also well-read and well-written, and your wisdom and genius left others smitten

The beauty and charm of a Royal Queen, many, especially your three children, hold you in the highest esteem

A woman of unparalleled wit, class and elegance, oh how God favored you with His Magnificence

You were a lover and a fighter at best; woe to the ones who put your love to the test

I always loved your ministry of correction, for it has provided for me a lifetime of protection

You were the best teacher and mentor to me, like to many, I hope to be

Whenever I saw you I kissed and hugged you countless times, somehow I always knew we'd run out of time

I remember how your beauty shone in your darkest hour, as our Father filled you with His Love, Peace and Power

My heart was broken into pieces when I knew you had to leave, and even now, after many years, it's still sometimes hard to believe

It brought me so much joy to be your daughter, and when you went home, I wondered how I'd face all my tomorrows

You told me that you'd always be with me but in a different way, You also told me to put my hand in God's Hand, and there let it stay

I love you with all my heart; I'm so glad that death will never keep us apart

In the coming years, as more children are born, I can't wait to tell them about their Nana, a beautiful rose among thorns

Mama, I will remember you always

....

Written By: PeriSean B. Hall, © July 12, 2010

*   *   *

Made in the USA
Charleston, SC
06 January 2015